Good Boundaries and Sex

How setting clear boundaries can improve your sex life

Margaret C. Taylor

CONTENT

CHAPTER ONE

Understanding Boundaries

Introduction

Any good relationship, including sexual interactions, must have boundaries. They are the boundaries we impose on ourselves and use to tell others around us what we will and won't put up with. Individual and situational boundaries may differ from one another and fluctuate based on a relationship or scenario. The idea of limits in relationships, their many varieties, and their connections to sexual encounters will all be covered in this chapter.

The Concept of Boundaries in Relationships

Boundaries, whether they be romantic or platonic, are the restrictions we place on ourselves in relationships. They are the invisible boundaries we draw around our bodies to express our wants, feelings, and personal boundaries. Boundaries are crucial for preserving successful relationships because they provide a secure environment where people may feel at ease, respected, and heard. They promote good communication and aid in building mutual trust between people, which may result in increased intimacy and emotional resiliency.

The Different Types of Boundaries

Relationship boundaries may take many various forms, and they range from person to person. Some individuals could have limits that are more strict than others, and vice versa. The following are a few examples of the many boundary kinds that people may establish:

1. bodily Boundaries: These restrictions apply to our bodily self and personal

space. They include topics including how near we can allow someone to approach us, how we like to be touched, and the kind of physical contact we are most at ease with.

2.   Emotional   Boundaries: These restrictions apply to our feelings and emotions. They include topics such as our emotional expression style, the feelings we feel safe disclosing, and the sort of emotional support we need from others.

3. Sexual Boundaries: These restrictions apply only to sexual encounters. They cover topics like our preferred sexual activities, our level of comfort with them,

and our unwillingness to engage in certain sexual activities.

4.   Intellectual Boundaries: These restrictions apply to our ideas, beliefs, and ways of thinking. They include issues including how we like to share ideas and perspectives, the kind of intellectual talks we find enjoyable, and the subjects we would rather avoid talking about.

5. Time Boundaries: These restrictions relate to our use of time and the activities we like. They include topics including how much time we like to spend with people, the kinds of activities we like to engage in, and the ones we don't want to engage in.

How Boundaries Relate to Sexual Experiences

Because they make people feel secure and respected, boundaries are crucial in sexual interactions. The restrictions that people place on themselves in sexual circumstances are known as sexual boundaries. They may discuss topics including the types of sexual conduct they are open to, the types they love, and the types they find objectionable.

Boundaries may be conveyed verbally, nonverbally, via body language, and explicitly through agreement. In sexual interactions, communication is essential.

People must be clear about their limits and respect those of their partners. People may create a secure environment where they can completely enjoy their sexual encounters without worrying about criticism or injury by establishing clear limits.

Any relationship, particularly a sexual one, requires an understanding of limits. Boundaries enable people to establish a secure environment where they may communicate their needs and wants and feel respected and heard. Verbal communication, nonverbal cues, and explicit agreement are just a few of the ways they may be expressed. Individuals may completely enjoy their sexual encounters and promote good communication and emotional connection with their partners by establishing clear limits.

How Setting Boundaries Can Enhance Your Sexual Life

For both people and the partnership as a whole, setting limits in sexual interactions may have a variety of advantages. Setting limits may enhance your sexual life in the following ways:

1. Increases Comfort and Safety: When people establish clear limits for

themselves and let their partner know about them, they build a feeling of security and comfort. As a result, they may enjoy themselves sexually without worrying about being judged or hurt.

2. Strengthens Communication: Effective boundary-setting calls for direct and honest communication between couples. People may establish a secure environment where they can freely express their wants and wishes by talking about their limitations and respecting those of others.

3. Promotes respect: By establishing limits, people demonstrate their regard

for both themselves and their spouses. Additionally, it demonstrates their concern for their partner's comfort and well-being, which may foster a stronger sense of respect and trust between the two of them.

4. Increases Pleasure: When people establish firm limits for themselves and share them with their partners, they are free to explore and completely appreciate their sexual experiences without worrying about criticism or injury. This may result in the relationship being more enjoyable and satisfying.

The Importance of Feeling Safe and Respected

In every sexual connection, feeling secure and valued is essential. When people are secure, they can completely relax and enjoy their intercourse. Greater emotional connection and closeness may result from making someone feel listened to, appreciated, and respected. By establishing a defined framework for their sexual encounters, boundaries may help people feel secure and appreciated.

How Boundaries Can Lead to Greater Intimacy and Connection

Intimacy and connection in sexual interactions may increase with the establishment of limits. When people respect each other's boundaries and explain their own, they provide a secure environment in which they may freely express their needs and wants. Increased emotional closeness and intimacy as a result of this open communication may improve the relationship's overall quality.

Any good sexual relationship must include the establishment of clear boundaries. Intimacy and connection may be increased, communication can be improved, and people can feel secure and appreciated by having a defined context for their sexual interactions. When people respect each other's boundaries and explain their own, they provide a secure environment in which they may freely express their needs and wants. As a result, the relationship may feel more pleasurable, content, and emotionally connected.

CHAPTER TWO

Identifying Your Boundaries

We'll look at how to recognize your limits and tell your partner about them. Setting boundaries involves being aware of your wants and limitations to make your relationship with your spouse safe and enjoyable for both of you.

How to Identify Your Boundaries

Since many of us have never taken the time to properly investigate our own needs and limitations, figuring out our boundaries may be difficult. The following

actions may help you define your
boundaries:

1. examine Your Past Experiences: Take
stock of your previous sexual encounters
and examine what went well and what
didn't. You may use this to find out where
limits might need to be established in the
future.

2. Think About Your Values: Your values
may guide you in establishing your limits.
You may need to establish limits for
communication and permission if, for
instance, you value honesty and trust.

3. Pay Attention to Your Body: When we feel uneasy or insecure, our bodies often provide us with signs. Recognize your limits by paying attention to how your body behaves throughout sexual situations.

Understanding Your Limits and Needs

Setting boundaries requires being aware of your needs and limitations. Here are some inquiries to think about while determining your demands and limitations:

What Levels of Comfort Do You Have? Think about what feels cozy and what doesn't. This may include conversation, sex, and physical contact.

2. What Needs Do You Have Emotionally? Take into account any emotional requirements you may have, such as the desire to be appreciated, cherished, or heard during a sexual encounter.

3. What Physical Needs Do You Have? Think about any physical requirements you have for breaks, protection, or to avoid particular postures during sex.

Communicating Your Boundaries Effectively

It's critical to successfully express your limits to your spouse once you've established your own. To communicate effectively, consider the following advice:

1. Be explicit and Clear: Express your limits in terms your spouse can understand, and be clear and explicit.

2. Use "I" words: Instead of criticizing or accusing your spouse, use "I" words to communicate your limits. Use the phrase "I feel uncomfortable with this" as opposed to "You make me uncomfortable."

3. Be Open to Negotiation: Be willing to talk with your spouse about your limits. You may need to take into account their demands and restrictions.

4. Listen to Your Partner: Be ready to respect your partner's boundaries and needs while paying attention to them with an open mind.

A safe and satisfying sexual encounter depends on you being aware of your limits and telling your partner about them. You may recognize your boundaries by thinking back on your prior encounters, taking into account your own beliefs, paying attention to your body, and being aware of your wants and limitations. A safe and respectful sexual encounter may be created for both you and your partner by properly communicating your limits to your partner using direct language and "I" statements, being open to negotiation, and paying attention to your partner's boundaries and needs.

Communicating Boundaries with Your Partner

The next stage is to successfully explain your limits to your spouse after you've established your own. Healthy relationships depend on open communication, and talking about limits with your partner may help to make sure that both of you feel secure, respected, and satisfied during sexual encounters.

How to Initiate a Conversation About Boundaries:

Although starting a discussion about limits might be scary, it is a crucial step in developing a positive and fulfilling sexual encounter. Here are some pointers for opening the discussion:

1. Pick the Right Time and Location: Decide on a time and location where you and your companion will feel relaxed and unbothered.

2. Use "I" words: Instead of blaming or assuming the worst about your spouse, use "I" words to convey your own needs and emotions.

3. Be straightforward and Honest: Be straightforward and honest when discussing your limits and the reasons behind their importance.

4. Ask for Consent: Before participating in sexual activity, ask your partner's permission and make sure they are at ease with any limits you establish.

Tips for Communicating Your Boundaries Effectively

For your limits to be accepted and preserved throughout sexual interactions, you must successfully communicate them. Here are some pointers for clearly stating your boundaries:

1. Be explicit and Clear: Express your limits in terms your spouse can understand, and be clear and explicit.

2. Use Positive Language: Instead of concentrating on what you don't want, use positive language to describe your

limits. For instance, use "I prefer" as opposed to "I don't like."

3. Be Firm and Forceful: When expressing your limits, be firm and forceful, and don't be hesitant to repeat them if required.

4. Offer Alternatives: Rather than just saying "no," offer alternatives or recommendations for activities that you find acceptable.

Responding to Your Partner's Boundaries

It's crucial to keep in mind that your spouse can also have limits they wish to express. The following advice can help you react to your partner's boundaries:

1. Listen Respectfully: Keep an open mind while you listen to your partner's limits and resist the urge to react defensively or dismissively.

2. Ask inquiries: Get to know your partner's wants and limits by asking inquiries.

3. Respect Their limits: Even if your spouse has different limits than you, respect theirs.

4. If Negotiation Is Required: If your partner's limits clash with yours, be willing to come to an agreement that benefits both of you.

The ability to establish and maintain limits during sexual interactions depends on effective communication. A safe and satisfying sexual encounter may be achieved by starting a talk about limits, properly conveying your boundaries, and reacting to your partner's boundaries. You may successfully express your limits with your partner and produce a happy sexual encounter for the two of you by utilizing "I" statements, being explicit and detailed, offering alternatives, and listening with respect.

CHAPTER THREE

Negotiating Boundaries Together

Setting limits is crucial for fostering a healthy and enjoyable sexual encounter, but it's also critical to acknowledge that everyone has their own unique set of boundaries. Setting limits with your partner may make sure that you both feel secure and respected and can make your sexual encounter more joyful overall. This chapter will cover boundary negotiations with your spouse, settling on a compromise that benefits both of you and periodically reviewing and modifying your limits.

How to Negotiate Boundaries with Your Partner

It takes the willingness to compromise, as well as open and honest communication, to negotiate limits in your relationship. The following advice can help you and your spouse negotiate boundaries:

1. Identify the Values You Share: To better comprehend each other's perspectives, talk about your common values and views towards sex and intimacy.

2. Recognize Each Other's Needs: Recognize each other's needs and limitations, and be prepared to make concessions when required.

3. Establish a Safe Space: Establish a negotiation-friendly environment where you both feel free to discuss your demands and limits.

4. Come up with solutions: Come up with answers that take into account your requirements as well as each other's limitations.

Finding a Middle Ground that Works for Both of You

A mutually beneficial compromise must be found while negotiating borders. Here are some pointers for locating a neutral position:

1. Put Respect First: Put respect for one another's needs and limits first.

2. Be Open-Minded: Be open-minded and prepared to take into account other viewpoints and concepts.

3. Concentrate on Finding Solutions Rather than Getting Stuck on the

Problem, Concentrate on Finding Solutions That Work for Both of You.

4. Create a strategy: Create a strategy for how you and your partner will continue to respect each other's needs and limits.

Revisiting and Adjusting Your Boundaries Over Time

It's crucial to periodically review and modify boundaries as needed since they might vary over time. Here are some pointers for periodically reviewing and modifying your boundaries:

1. Check-In often: Communicate with one another often to see if any boundaries have changed or should be modified.

2. Be Flexible: Be adaptable and prepared to change your limits as needed.

3. Communicate modifications: Be courteous and explicit when letting your spouse know about any boundary modifications.

4. Respect Each Other's Changes: Even if your boundaries have changed, respect each other's changes in boundaries.

Negotiating boundaries with your partner requires open and honest communication, a willingness to compromise, and a focus on finding a middle ground that works for both of you. You may have a satisfying and healthy sexual encounter with your partner by emphasizing respect, being open-minded, concentrating on solutions, and developing a plan for how you will respect one another's limits going ahead. Additionally, it's critical to periodically review and modify your limits and to politely and clearly explain any adjustments to your spouse.

Overcoming Challenges to Boundaries

While establishing and maintaining limits may significantly enhance your sexual encounters, doing so can sometimes be difficult. In this chapter, we'll look at some typical problems individuals run into while trying to establish and maintain boundaries, as well as solutions. We'll also talk about how crucial it is to take care of oneself and get help when you need it.

Common Challenges to Setting and Maintaining Boundaries

People often encounter the following difficulties while establishing and maintaining boundaries:

1. worry of Rejection: If someone expresses their limits, they could worry that their partner will reject them.

2. Guilt or Shame: People may experience guilt or shame for establishing boundaries, particularly if they have been taught that their wants and needs are unimportant.

3. Pressure to comply: Even when cultural standards for sex and intimacy clash with an individual's limits, people may nevertheless feel under pressure to comply.

4. Communication Issues: People often find it difficult to express their limits clearly, which may cause confusion or misunderstandings.

Strategies for Overcoming Challenges

To overcome these obstacles, it's crucial to

1. Prioritize self-awareness: Recognize your needs and limits as well as any anxieties or preconceived notions that can prevent you from establishing and maintaining boundaries.

2. Exercise Self-Compassion: Recognize that it's acceptable to have anxiety or unease while establishing boundaries, and exercise self-compassion whenever these emotions surface.

3. Communicate Clearly: To make sure that your limits are recognized, use effective communication techniques including employing "I" statements and active listening.

4. Set Realistic Expectations: Avoid creating limits that are excessively strict or unyielding by being realistic about what you may expect from your spouse and yourself.

5. Seek Support: Ask for help in establishing and maintaining boundaries from friends, family members, or a therapist.

The Importance of Self-Care and Seeking Support

It may be emotionally difficult to establish and maintain limits, so it's important to prioritize self-care and get help when you need it. Some methods for taking care of oneself and getting assistance include:

1. Self-Care: Take part in self-care-promoting activities, such as working out, practicing meditation, or spending time with loved ones.

2. Seek Support: Ask for help in establishing and maintaining boundaries

from friends, family members, or a therapist.

3. Practice Being Assertive: To gain confidence in establishing and upholding boundaries, practice being assertive in other aspects of your life, such as at work or in social settings.

4. Establish limits with Support: Establish limits with the assistance of a therapist, a dependable friend, or a family member who can assist you in overcoming any difficulties.

Although it may be difficult to establish and maintain limits, doing so is crucial to having satisfying and healthy sexual encounters. Prioritizing self-awareness, self-compassion, effective communication, reasonable expectations, and seeking help when necessary are crucial for overcoming typical barriers to defining and maintaining boundaries. Developing assertiveness abilities and practicing self-care may both aid in maintaining limits. Keep in mind to emphasize respect and understanding in all facets of your sexual encounters and to be patient with both yourself and your partner.

Beyond Boundaries: Other Factors That Impact Your Sex Life

There are additional elements that might affect your sex life in addition to establishing and keeping boundaries, which are crucial for developing good sexual encounters. We will examine some of these elements in this chapter, such as permission and communication, and how they fit into the overall picture of healthy sexual interactions. We'll also provide advice on how to keep enhancing your sex life.

Other Factors That Impact Your Sex Life:

1.   Communication: Healthy sexual encounters depend on effective communication. Greater intimacy and connection may result from being able to communicate your needs, wants, and limits as well as hear what your spouse has to say and react to it. You may explore new sexual sensations and prevent misconceptions or discomfort by communicating with one another.

2. Consent: The foundation of wholesome sexual encounters is consent. It denotes

that both parties have provided their explicit, informed agreement to engage in sexual activity and are eager and willing participants. A safe and satisfying sexual encounter must be created, and this requires both parties to understand consent, be able to communicate and respect one another's limits.

3. Trust: For satisfying sexual encounters, trust is also crucial. Intimacy and connection may be fostered when couples feel comfortable and confident with one another. Effective communication, honesty, and respect for one another's limits are all ways to develop trust.

4. Emotional Connection: Healthy sexual relationships also depend on strong emotional connections. A deeper degree of intimacy and connection may develop between you and your spouse if you can communicate your thoughts, emotions, and experiences. Effective communication, quality time spent together, and the development of empathy and understanding are all ways to strengthen an emotional connection.

5. Self-Care: Taking good care of your body and mind may also affect how you feel about sex. Making self-care a priority may make you feel more certain, at ease, and present during sexual activities.

Examples of self-care practices include getting adequate sleep, eating properly, and controlling stress.

Tips for Improving Your Sex Life

1. Communicate Effectively: Work on your communication techniques, including active listening and expressing your wants and limits using "I" statements.

2. Demonstrate permission: Recognize the value of permission in sexual activities, respect it, and talk openly with your partner to make sure that both of you are at ease and willing participants.

3. Establish Trust: Establish trust with your spouse by being honest, open-minded, and respectful of one another's limits.

4. Prioritize Emotional Connection: Make emotional connection a top priority by talking to your spouse about your emotions and experiences, spending time with each other, and developing empathy and understanding.

5. Prioritize Self-Care: To feel more certain, at ease, and present during sexual activities, prioritize self-care activities like getting adequate sleep, eating healthily, and controlling stress.

6. Explore New Experiences: To guarantee a safe and happy encounter, be open to exploring new sexual experiences with your partner and express your wishes and limits openly.

7. Seek Help When Needed: If you need advice or support from a therapist or medical expert on any element of your sexual encounters, do so.

Conclusion

There are additional elements that might affect your sex life in addition to creating and keeping boundaries, which are essential components of successful sexual encounters. The creation of satisfying and joyful sexual encounters depends on effective communication, permission, trust, emotional connection, and self-care. You can keep improving your sex life and enhancing your connection with your spouse by using these techniques and being open to trying new things. In all facets of your sexual encounters, keep in mind that respect, communication, and understanding are priorities.